Collector's Guide to Country Stoneware & Pottery
Second Series

by
Don and Carol Raycraft

COLLECTOR BOOKS
A Division of Schroeder Publishing Co., Inc.

The current values in this book should be used only as a guide. They are not intended to set prices, which vary from one section of the country to another. Auction prices as well as dealer prices vary greatly and are affected by condition as well as demand. Neither the Author nor the Publisher assumes responsibility for any losses that might be incurred as a result of consulting this guide.

Acknowledgments

Al Behr
Bill Grande
Ann and Tom Hixson
Steve Rhodes
Elmer and Merrilyn Fedder
Alex Hood
Mary Burgess
Howie and Iris Hirsch
Judy Judd
Eve Wilson
Kevin and Debbie Shimansky

Linda Moor Anelli
Roy and Pat Buncher
Byron and Sara Dillow
Marie Bozinovich
Michael Sheets
Opel and Joe Pickens
Barry and Lisa McAllister
Greg and Ella Cummins
Bon Aqua Pottery
Al and Barb Blumberg
Jim White

Photography

Carol Raycraft
R. Craig Raycraft
Ann Hixson
Elmer Fedder
Greg Cummins
Roy Ferris

George Bolster
Al Behr
Steve Thackrey
Lisa McAllister
Al Blumberg

Contents

Stoneware Chronology

1500-1700 – Stoneware was being produced in numerous potteries in England and Germany.

1500s – Cobalt was first used to decorate stoneware in German potteries.

1639 – Several potters moved to Essex County, Mass.; by 1775 more than 75 potteries are in operation in the area.

1671 – John Dwight of Fulham, England patented a salt-glazing process.

1735 – Redware potteries in Pennsylvania are in operation.

1793 – Bennington, Vermont pottery is in business. It continues until 1894 under numerous combinations of ownership.

1840 – The American Pottery Manufacturing Company (Jersey City, N.J.) issued its first transfer printed table ware and an octagonal pitcher with a portrait of William Henry Harrison.

1840s – The number of rural potteries declined rapidly with the improvement of the road and canal system in the United States and larger potteries secured a greater share of the market.

1845 – Rockingham glazed stoneware pitchers, candlesticks and "book" flasks are popular. Many are made at potteries in Vermont and Ohio.

1860s (late) – The market for stoneware canning jars is diminished by the development of glass jars.

1870 – The peak period of brush-decorated stoneware.

1875 – The stoneware industry continues to lose business to technological innovations like home refrigeration with the development of ice boxes.

1885 – Mass produced, inexpensive glass jars and bottles are commonly available. This development takes away even more of the stoneware market.

1890 – Bristol glazed tops and Albany slip bottoms are found on much midwestern molded stoneware.

1890-1920 – Bristol glaze was in common use in most midwestern stoneware potteries.

1900 – A few potteries in eastern Pennsylvania and Ohio are still making redware. A U.S. government report indicates the state produced $400,000 worth of redware and more than $1,000,000 worth of stoneware in 1900.

1910 – The salt glazed stoneware industry has almost ceased to exist in the United States.

1918 – Lenox Inc. supplies the first American-made ceramic table service to the White House.

1925 – For all practical purposes, the American stoneware industry is dead.

Introduction

In 1939, John Ramsey's classic book, *American Potters and Pottery*, was published. One of Ramsey's primary objectives was to provide information about the identification and location of 19th century American potters. This was a difficult and tedious task because there was no central data source for the information.

There were hundreds of potteries in and out of business in the eastern United States between 1800 and 1850. Many were "blue-bird" potters who worked only in the summer and served a local area with their limited production of wares. Most of their crocks, jugs and churns were not marked and little information about the makers survives.

Potters were notoriously bad businessmen who focused most of their attention on the production of stoneware or redware and managing their kilns. Inevitably there was a kiln explosion or fire that put them out of business. The pottery at Bennington, Vermont is considered to be among the most stable of all American operations because it produced high-quality stoneware that ranged from table ware to picture frames for more than a century. It is interesting to note that the Bennington pottery went through at least 12 changes in ownership during the 19th century. The longest single period of stability was from 1861-1881 when it carried the mark of E. and L.P. Norton.

Most potteries were located in rural areas because of the constant threat of fire and explosion, and the chlorine and hydrochloric acid fumes given off during the firing process. Much of the typical stoneware potteries' business was local up to the late 1840s when the opening of the Erie Canal and improved highways brought significant change. Clay was expensive to transport and stoneware crocks and jugs didn't travel well in horse-drawn wagons over roads that were paved with holes and ruts.

As the quality of travel improved and the Erie Canal opened new markets, much larger factories that mass-produced stoneware took over from the local potter with only a few employees. The local potteries could not compete and soon went out of business.

Note: The stoneware items with taped prices on the pages that follow were originally offered for sale in the early 1970s. With the resurgence of interest over the past 15 years in decorated stoneware, the prices of these items have escalated several times.

The pictures with prices are from the files of Al Behr. Mr. Behr publishes a periodic catalog of stoneware for sale. Over the years, he has shipped hundreds of pieces throughout America.

For additional information, you may write to him at R.D. 8, Horsepound Road, Carmel, New York 10512.

Collecting Stoneware

Today many collectors are especially interested in decorated pieces of salt-glazed stoneware. The decoration ranges from simple swirls or brushed capacity marks to elaborate animals, flowers, and human figures.

John Ramsey wrote that "The collector must discriminate, avoiding both an assembledge of common and uninteresting perfect pieces, and an assortment of cracked or otherwise damaged examples of fine ware."

If you want a collection of perfect pieces of stoneware, visits to antique shops, shows, flea markets, malls and yard sales will probably result in a room full of early 20th century mass-produced jugs and jars without cracks, chips or blemishes of any kind.

If you want a collection of jugs and jars that have been decorated by hand and turned individually on a potter's wheel more than a century ago, you may have to accept a periodic chip, minor crack or kiln blemish to accomplish your mission. The size of the check will be dramatically larger.

More than 50 years ago Ramsey wrote, "Much really beautiful and fine ware was made for hard everyday use, and unless by some lucky accident it has escaped that use, it is bound to show some scars." He mentioned that the "fetishes of present-day (1939) collecting" were pieces in perfect condition that were also marked by their maker.

The stoneware that is illustrated on the pages that follow is primarily utilitarian and not ornamental. It was made to be used on a daily basis. It was inexpensive and readily available. If a piece was cracked to the point that it wasn't water tight, it was thrown away because it could not be repaired as simply as something made of wood or metal.

The three classifications of pottery below are among the most sought after today by Americana collectors:

Stoneware

1. Began to be made in quantity in small potteries after 1800.
2. Stoneware was decorated with the following techniques:
   a. incising – a process of scratching a design into the stoneware with a pointed rod or sharp nail. Little incising was done after 1845.
   b. free hand with a brush dipped in cobalt – brush decoration ranges from simple swirls and numbers to highly complex scenes involving animals, buildings and vegetation. The "golden age" of brush decorating was during the 1865-1875 period.
   c. free hand with slip-cup – slip-cupping involves pouring a thin line of slip out of a "cup" and producing birds, flowers, business names, swirls or animals. The "cup" was often made of clay with quills that served as pouring spouts. Slip-

cups were in use from about 1830-1880.
   d. stenciling – with the mechanization of the stoneware industry after 1880, most stoneware was labeled or decorated by stenciling. Canning jars from western Pennsylvania that date as early as the 1860s were often heavily stenciled and also decorated with a brush.
3. The clays used in the production of stoneware were finer and more dense than common redware clays and pieces were fired to at least 2100 degrees Fahrenheit. The stoneware was fired to the point of vitrification so the finished wares would absorb no water.
4. Stoneware was popular because it was durable and could be easily cleaned. It was ideal for food storage because it was water tight and left no taste or flavor on its contents. The glaze was safe and did not contaminate food.
5. There were hundreds of local, regional, and national stoneware potteries throughout the 19th century, but by 1925 almost all were closed. The stoneware industry suffered a series of major setbacks with the development of inexpensive glass bottles and jars, factory-made home ice boxes and Prohibition, which outlawed the sale of alcohol, also ended the market for stoneware beer bottles.
6. There is not documentation, but it is an excellent bet that the closer in proximity stoneware potteries were during the 19th century, the more likely they were to elaborately decorate their wares to gain a competitive edge. The most skillfully-decorated pieces probably came from areas that had numerous competing potteries within the same region.
7. The salt that was thrown into the kiln at the height of the firing process vaporized and turned into a fog that settled over and glazed the stacked contents of the kiln. The salt glaze left the surface of the stoneware with the appearance of an orange peel and served as a final coating of protection.
8. It has been our experience that dealers who specialize in stoneware and related antiques are usually most aware of what they have and price it accordingly. A dealer who purchases an estate and finds six crocks in the basement often tends to price the pieces at an extreme. They are either very inexpensive or marked three times what they are worth.

   Dealers who buy and sell stoneware on a regular basis have an appreciation for what makes a particular piece common or rare and its approximate value in an ever-changing market.
9. In evaluating a piece of stoneware most collectors are concerned with the following:
   a. condition – if a three-gallon crock from Ft. Edward, N.Y. has a single cobalt flower and a

complex crack, most collectors will show little interest. If the three-gallon crock from Ft. Edward has a cobalt lion standing inside a fence with three pine trees and a complex crack, there will still be a line of willing collectors with checkbooks in hand.

b. decoration – birds, animals, buildings, human figures, and ships add significant value to stoneware. A stoneware jug is a stoneware jug unless it has a great deal of cobalt decoration. At that point, it becomes a piece of American folk art.

c. mark – to many collectors, the potter's mark is the least important of the four criteria described here. Some serious collectors have heart palpatations when they hear names like Paul Cushman, Remmey, Crolius, Commeraw, Caire, and Stetzenmeyer.

d. form – a piece of stoneware that is pear-shaped or ovoid normally dates before 1850. After that date, pieces became increasingly more cylindrical in form.

Yellowware

1. Yellowware pitchers, plates, serving platters, mugs and bowls were manufactured in huge quantities during the 19th and early 20th centuries.
2. Yellowware is covered with a clear or colorless glaze which enhances the natural color of the clay. Yellowware was almost always molded rather than thrown on a wheel and is seldom marked with the maker's name.
3. Between 1830 and 1900, yellowware was made in more than 80 potteries from New England to Illinois. There were still potteries as late as 1940 making yellowware.

4. Yellowware doorstops, pitchers and candlesticks were made in numerous midwestern potteries that also made Rockingham items. Often the same molds were used for Rockingham and yellowware.
5. The arca around East Liverpool, Ohio was found to contain a wealth of yellow clays that was ideal for producing yellowware as early as the late 1840s. The Roseville Pottery Company, that is more famous for its art pottery, was making yellowware for American consumers in 1901.

Redware

1. Redware pottery was made from surface-dug clays that produced a soft, fragile, and porous ware that was usually covered by a colorless lead glaze. The lead glaze was a silent killer for many 19th century citizens of Pennsylvania because it bled into its contents when exposed to some food and liquids stored inside.
2. Redware was rarely signed and was produced in quantity from about 1630 until as late as 1900 in some isolated areas. By 1850, the surviving redware potteries were in rural areas and were making flower pots and field tiles rather than jugs and crocks.
3. White slip was used to decorate pie plates in Pennsylvania and manganese oxide produced a black metallic color for tea pots and tea sets. Copper filings were used to make a green glaze. If a potter used cobalt in the mix, he ended up with an expensive black glaze that was more commonly and economically achieved with manganese.
4. Most American redware, with the exception of pie plates and flower pots, was hand thrown on a wheel rather than molded.

Producing Decorated Stoneware

To gain some insight into how stoneware crocks and jugs are made, we have called upon two prominent potters, Al and Barbara Blumberg. The Blumbergs operate a small studio pottery in their middle Tennessee home. They combine their art backgrounds and a love for 19th century folk pottery to produce traditional salt-glazed stoneware. Al makes the pots and Barbara does most of the decorating, and they collaborate on the designing of shapes and patterns.

Although the studio is not open to the public, information about the availability of their wares may be secured by sending a self-addressed, stamped envelope to the Bon Aqua Pottery, Route 1, Box 396-10, Bon Aqua, Tennessee 37025.

There is much confusion about how pottery is produced. Most people expect a truly handmade piece of stoneware to be one which was turned on a potter's wheel and decorated by the artist's hand. Many collectors are disappointed to find that some pieces in their collections were actually made by jigger-molds, ram-presses, or slip casting molds and decorated by stencils, rubber stamps or decals.

made by different potters reflect the techniques and style of the individual craftsman. In contrast, the production of pottery using industrial molds can be taught to a beginner in a few hours or days and the finished product will be

The use of a potter's wheel, like a musical instrument, takes years of practice to master. No two pieces made by the same potter are exactly alike, and similar pots

uniform; showing no variation from piece to piece, or potter to potter. An experienced potter can make over 100 pieces per day on the wheel, while an unskilled worker can make over 1,000 pots on a ram-press in the same amount of time.

The use of mass production techniques is not a recent development. Toward the later half of the 19th century, inexpensive glass containers became common-place to American consumers. Traditional potteries began shifting towards industrial methods in order to stay competitive in a changing market. Potters were replaced by molds and machinery, and decorators were traded for stamps and stencils. Most historians and collectors agree that by the turn of the 20th century, traditional utilitarian stoneware had lost most of its aesthetic appeal.

Clay is the basic ingredient in the production of all

pottery. It can be found on every continent, for it is one of the most abundant materials present on this planet. Clay is actually decomposed rock, which was formed over millions of years through the erosion action of wind, water,

heat and cold. Potters can dig their own clay or purchase commercially-mined clays and blend them to create a desired clay body. Moist, pre-mixed clay bodies can also be obtained from commercial suppliers.

The process begins with the determination of the clay to be used. A particular clay is selected based on the type of pottery to be made. Earthenware clay is used to produce redware because its low melting point is suitable for the lower temperatures of a redware firing. Stoneware clay has a much higher melting point, which is necessary for the high temperatures required to fire stoneware. The color of clay can be controlled to obtain certain effects. Some potters select relatively pure clays to create pottery which has a white or cream-colored body. Others may choose a clay high in iron or even add oxide to their clay to give the clay body a rich, brown color. At Bon Aqua Pottery, we have developed our own clay formula for the production of salt-glazed stoneware. It is a light-colored clay, suitable for stoneware temperatures and is capable of attracting a good salt glaze coating in the kiln.

Once the clay has been mixed to the proper consistency, it must be prepared before forming it on the wheel. First, rough clay balls are formed and precisely weighed to pre-determined sizes according to the particular pots to be made. Next, we wedge each piece of clay by hand to remove pockets of air inside the clay. This process is similar to kneading dough for baking bread.

The clay ball is placed in the center of the wheelhead to begin forming the pot. While the ball is turning at high speed, pressure from the potter's hands bear down on the clay, centering it perfectly on the wheel. Both thumbs are pressed into the center of the clay, forming a doughnut shape. With one hand inside the doughnut and the other hand outside, even pressure forces the clay wall upward. This process is repeated until the pot reaches the desired size and shape. Grooves appear in the side of the pot where pressure from the finger tips squeezed the clay. We use a small, flat, wooden tool called a "rib" to smooth out these grooves on the outer surface of each pot. Finger marks are left on the inside walls and can be seen on our fired ware. Pottery buyers can look for these marks on any pottery to help determine whether a certain piece is wheel thrown or not. A wire is pulled across the bottom of the pot to free it from the wheel head. The piece is carefully picked up and placed on a board to dry. Fingerprints are often left in the soft clay and sometimes can be seen on the fired pots. It is intriguing to find stoneware made over 100 years ago with fingerprints as fresh as the day they were made.

After the pots have air-dried for a day or so, they become firm enough to pick up without bending out of shape. This "leather hard" stage is when we apply handles and finish the pot. Like the pots, each handle is com-

pletely handmade. A piece of clay is attached to the pot and repeatedly stroked or hand pulled to form the desired size and shape for each handle. After this process, the pottery mark and capacity mark are impressed on the ware.

After the pottery has dried further, we coat the inside of each piece with "true" Albany slip glaze. American salt-glazed stoneware has relied on this rich brown glaze for about two centuries. In the spring of 1987 Albany slip went out of production forever. Potters using "true" Albany slip glaze today will have to rely on stockpiles or find some way of digging it themselves.

Next, the pottery is decorated with cobalt blue slip. The slip we use in our decorations is not paint, but actually liquid clay with cobalt oxide mixed in it. When it is applied to the green pottery and fired in the kiln, it becomes part of the pot, you can't wash or scratch it off.

Decorating pottery with clay slip is not like drawing on paper. The surface is soft and curved and you cannot easily erase your mistakes. The designs are applied free hand, no stencils are used to decorate the pots. Several traditional techniques are used to apply the blue slip. Some pots are decorated with a brush, some with a slip trailer, and others are a combination of both. On rare occasions, designs are incised into the clay with a sharp stick and then filled in with cobalt slip.

After the pottery has thoroughly dried, each piece is carefully loaded into the kiln and the firing process begins. The temperature in the kiln begins to rise very slowly at first. Approximately 24 hours later, the kiln is at the right temperature for salting. This is a critical moment because any mistakes made at this point can jeopardize the appearance of the entire kiln load. Salt is scattered throughout the kiln and allowed to circulate so the pots are evenly coated. Twenty-four to 48 hours later, the kiln is cool enough to be unloaded.

All stoneware made by Bon Aqua Pottery is salt fired. Historically, salt-glazed stoneware came in many colors and shades. The color of our clay fires from a light grey to a creamy beige, similar in color to pottery produced in New York and New England during the 19th century. This primitive process creates tonal variations and flashing similar to that seen on old pots. These subtle ranges in color and the unpredictability of the salt-glaze process lends an excitement to each firing and assures that each piece of pottery produced is one of a kind.

Grande Collection

Several of the more elaborately decorated pieces of stoneware in this book are from the collection of Bill Grande. Mr. Grande operates the Regent Street Antique Center at 153 Regent Street, Saratoga Springs, New York 12866. The Regent Street Antique Center contains 11,000 square feet of antiques offered for sale by 30 dealers. It is open daily from 10:00 a.m. until 5:00 p.m.

The Center also houses a private museum with displays of Hummels, scrimshaw, canes, bells, and a world class collection of decorated stoneware.

Jugs

Left:
Lyons, N.Y. two-gallon jug, brushed flower, c. mid-19th century.

Right:
Four-gallon jug, E. & L.P. Norton, Bennington, Vt. 1861-1881.

Right:
Early ocher flowering tree or large plant on L. Norton, Bennington, Vt., jug, 1828-1833.

Left:
Jacob Caire, Poughkeepsie, N.Y., two-gallon jug with deep cobalt brushed decoration, c. 1850.

Right:
Three-gallon jug with elaborate scene and deer, slip trailed, Whites Utica, N.Y.

Left:
Bird of prey in cobalt on three-gallon jug from J. & E. Norton, Bennington, Vt., 1850-1861.

Left:
Three-gallon jug from Whites Utica, double pheasants in a tree, slip-trailed, c. 1870's.

Right:
William Roberts, Binghamton, N.Y., c. 1870's jug with slip-trailed flower.

Left:
Three-gallon ovoid jug, c. 1840's, cobalt decoration, incised capacity mark.

Right:
Ottman Bros., Ft. Edward, N.Y. 1876, "Centennial," man drinking on a keg.

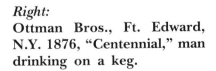

Above:
19th century molasses "pitcher jugs" with Albany slip glaze.

Left:
Two-gallon vendor's jug, Theodore Philips, Buffalo, N.Y., Bristol glaze, c. 1900, stenciled label.

Above:
**Impressed vendor's label on
Poland Mineral Spring Water
five-gallon jug, c. 1880's.**

Right:
**"Running" bird slip-trailed on
two-gallon Whites Utica jug.**

18

Right:
**Clark and Fox, Athens, N.Y.,
ovoid jug, c. 1830's.**

Below:
**Jugs with similar deep cobalt
flower decorations, c. 1860's.**

Left:
Two-gallon "bird" jug, N.Y. state, c. 1870's.

Below:
One-gallon jug.
Two-gallon jug with brushed flowers.
One-gallon vendor's jug, Hollenbeck Bros., Catskill, N.Y.

Left:
Unusual ovoid jug with brushed flower and stenciled letters, c. 1840's.

Right:
Unmarked jug with cobalt flower, probably N.Y. state, c. 1870's.

Left:
Cobalt flowers on jug from the late 1880's.

Below:
Norton and Fenton, Bennington, Vt. one-gallon jug, 1843-47 mark.

Above:
One-gallon vendor's jug, c. 1890.

One-gallon vendor's jug, impressed capacity and maker's mark, West Troy, N.Y., c. 1880.

Right:
Two-gallon jug with slip-trailed decoration, c. 1880's.

Right:
Unusual three-gallon jug, dated, flowers formed in the shape of a heart, possibly a gift on a birthday or anniversary.

Below:
Three vendor's jugs from the late 19th century:
–impressed "William Hayes" from New Hampshire
–stenciled label from Buffalo, N.Y.
–brushed label from liquor dealer

Left:
Early 19th century stoneware jug with impressed or stamped decoration.

Below:
Two heavily decorated jugs from the D.L. and A.K. Ballard Pottery, Burlington, Vt., c. 1860's.

Right:
Floral spray decorated two-gallon jug from N.Y. state, c. 1870's.

Left:
Goodwin and Webster ovoid jug from Hartford, Conn., c. 1840.

Above:
Four-gallon unmarked jug dated "1848."

Left:
Sidney Risley jug from Norwich, Conn., c. 1840's.

Left:
Two-gallon "F. Woodward" jug with deep cobalt leaf decoration, c. mid-19th century.

Right:
Ovoid jug with brushed cobalt flower, c. 1840's.

Above:
Knapp and Allen vendor's pitcher jug from Red Bank, N.J., c. 1900.

Left:
Sponge decorated molded maple syrup jug with "drop" handle, c. early 1900's.

Left:
Five-gallon molded "platform" or "porch" jug, midwestern, c. early 1900's.

Below:
Contemporary "face" or "grotesque" jugs.

30

Right:
E. and L.P. jug, Bennington, Vt., 1861-1881, cobalt leaf.

Left:
Five-gallon vendor's jug, Bristol glaze, c. 1900.

Above:
Miniature stoneware jugs from southwestern Illinois, c. early 1900s.

Below:
Dated pieces of American stoneware are not common. These examples were found in North Carolina.

Right:
Patriotic scenes are extremely rare. This incised ship on an ovoid jug dates from the 1810-1840 period and was made at the N. Clark and Company Pottery, Athens, N.Y.

Left:
Most potters applied handles to their pieces after the pots had air dried for several days.

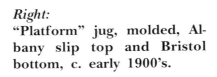

Left:
Pennsylvania vendor's jug, Bristol bottom, c. early 1900's.

Right:
"Platform" jug, molded, Albany slip top and Bristol bottom, c. early 1900's.

Right:
Molded mineral spring jug with "drop" handle, c. early 1900's.

Left:
Molded whiskey vendor's jug from Kentucky, stenciled label, c. early 1900's.

Crocks

Left:
Four-gallon crock from Ft. Edward, N.Y., double "love bird" pheasants perched on a stump.

Right:
"Dragon fly" crock, c. 1870's, Jacob Fisher, Lyons, N.Y.

Right:
Five-gallon crock, prancing 14-point deer, tree stump, and fence scene, Haxstun, Ottman and Company.

Below:
Twenty-five gallon stoneware crock, slip-trailed flower, midwestern, c. 1890.

Left:
Four-gallon crock, Ballard, Burlington, Vt., deep cobalt bird.

Right:
C.W. Braun, Buffalo, N.Y., c. 1860's, turkey with wing and feathers made up of more than 100 cobalt blue dots.

Right:
Four-gallon midwestern crock, slip-trailed inverted Christmas tree, c. 1880's.

2

SAM EDWARDS,
Cash Grocer,
CARROLLTON, ILLINOIS.

Left:
Two-gallon vendor's crock, Bristol glaze, Illinois, c. 1900.

Right:
"Bird" crock, probably N.Y. state, c. 1870's.

Left:
Rare running elephant on three-gallon crock, West Troy, New York.

42

Right:
20th-century midwestern crock, Bristol glaze, stenciled decoration.

Below:
Two-gallon crock with cobalt dragon fly.
Three-gallon N.Y. state crock with cobalt slip-trailed flower, c. 1870's.
Three-gallon midwestern crock with cobalt swirl, c. 1880's.

Above:
A.K. Ballard, Burlington, Vt., two-gallon jar, c. 1870's. Unmarked two-gallon crock with brushed leaf, c. 1870's.

Left:
Midwestern two-gallon crock with brushed capacity mark and simple decoration, c. 1890.

Left:
Late 19th-century four-gallon crock, brushed decoration, found in Kentucky.

Below:
Adam Caire, Poughkeepsie, N.Y., three-gallon crock, c. 1870's.

Heavily decorated crock with cobalt floral spray.

Right:
Five-gallon crock, cobalt butter fly, slip-trailed, c. 1880.

Left:
Slip-trailed flower, unmarked, N.Y. state, c. 1880.

Left:
Four-gallon "chicken pecking corn," N.Y. state, c. 1870's.

Right:
Three-gallon, unmarked, "chicken pecking corn," N.Y. state, c. 1870's.

49

Left:
Brushed flower on unmarked crock, c. 1870's.

Below:
Four-gallon crock from Lyons, N.Y. c. 1870's.

Right:
Two-gallon deep cobalt "bird" crock, c. early twentieth century.

Right:
Two-gallon deep cobalt "bird" crock, c. early twentieth century.

Above:
Stenciled Pennsylvania preserve jar, c. 1880's.

Brushed dragon fly crock, c. 1870's.

Left:
Unusually decorated crock in deep cobalt from the late 19th century.

Above Left:
Four-gallon midwestern crock, slip-trailed inverted Christmas tree, c. 1900.

Above Right:
Two-gallon Poughkeepsie crock with cobalt floral spray, c. 1870's.

Left:
Fifteen-gallon midwestern crock, c. early 1900's.

Left:
Unmarked crock, probably New York state in origin with brushed flower or plant, c. 1880.

Right:
Late 19th-century two-gallon crock, stenciled capacity mark.

Jars

Right:
1½-gallon stoneware jar with stenciled capacity mark and decoration, c. 1880's.

Left:
Unmarked jar, double handles, c. late 19th century, English in origin.

Above:
**Whites Utica two-gallon jar with cobalt flower.
Unmarked decorated jar, probably Bennington, VT., c. 1850's.**

Right:
Incised flower on unmarked jar, c. 1830's.

Right:
New York state jar with brushed decoration, c. 1850.

Left:
Incised swags and pendants on unmarked ovoid jar, c. 1830.

Left:
Two gallon semi-ovoid crock, A.O. Whittemore, Havana, New York, slip-trailed trout, c. 1860's.

Right:
Unmarked, brush decorated jar, c. 1840's.

Above:
Stoneware fruit or preserve jar, unmarked, c. 1870's.

Early 19th century fruit or preserve jar, brush decoration around the rim.

Left:
Brush-decorated jar, c. 1870's.

Left:
Unmarked jar, simple cobalt decoration, c. 1840's.

Below:
Sponge-decorated molded jars, c. 1900, midwestern.

Right:
Unmarked early 19th-century ovoid jar, brush decoration of a leaf.

Left:
Olean, N.Y. three-gallon jar with cobalt leaves and flowers, c. 1870's.

Right:
The handles of this jug have been enhanced by a splash of cobalt.

Below:
Midwestern stoneware jars, Albany slip, late 19th century.

Above:
Redware apple butter jars, Pennsylvania, c. 1860-1880.

Below:
1½-gallon bowl from Sipe and Son, Williams Port, Pennsylvania, c. 1860's.

Left:
Caire Pottery, Poughkeepsie, N.Y., c. 1840's, jar with cobalt decoration.

Right:
Brushed flowers on stoneware jar, New York state, c. mid-19th century.

64

Right:
Crolius Pottery, New York City, c. 1830's, decorated jar.

Left:
Unmarked stoneware jar, brushed leaf, c. 1830's.

Water Coolers

Right:
Bennington Factory, c. 1820, four-gallon cooler, decorated with a brushed tree and a splash of cobalt by each "ear."

Left:
Early 20th-century three-gallon stoneware cooler with Bristol glaze and cobalt stripes.

Left:
Early 20th-century three-gallon stoneware cooler with Bristol glaze.

Below:
Ovoid unmarked stoneware cooler, double handles, brushed capacity mark and "lion," found in Kentucky but probably from New York state, c. 1830's.

Left:
It is interesting to speculate how an ovoid, utilitarian cooler with fragile double handles could exist for more than 150 years and retain its original condition while making its way from New York to rural Kentucky.

Molded "platform" cooler with double handles and Albany slip glaze, c. 1900.

Butter Churns

Above:
Albany slip stoneware butter churn, probably midwestern in origin, c. 1900.
Four-gallon cobalt decorated butter churn, c. 1860's-1870's.

Left:
Five-gallon churn from T. Harrington, Lyons, New York, c. 1852-1872.
The eight-pointed starburst surrounds the face of a jockey with a cap.

Left:
**Five-gallon churn from E. &
L.P. Norton, Bennington,
Vermont, 1861-1881.**

Right:
**Six-gallon butter churn
marked "Jordan" with a slip-
trailed bird decoration.**

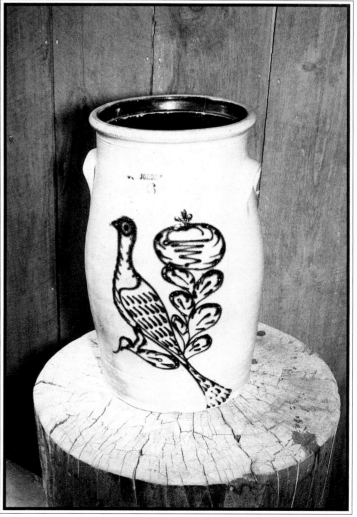

71

Left:
Ottman Brothers and Company, Fort Edward, N.Y., five-gallon churn with detailed deer and flying ducks.

Right:
Unmarked stoneware churn, c. 1880.

Right:
Unmarked five-gallon churn with unusual brushed decoration.

Left:
Ovoid stoneware churn, c. 1830's.

Right:
Three-gallon butter churn with cobalt decoration, c. 1880's.

Left:
Four-gallon Red Wing butter churn, Bristol glaze, c. early 20th century.

Rockingham

Left:
Yellow earthenware plate with Rockingham glaze, unmarked, c. 1880.

Below:
Yellow earthenware mixing bowl with Rockingham glaze, unmarked, c. 1880.

Above:
Molded storage jar for tobacco, yellow earthenware with Rockingham glaze, unmarked, c. 1850-1880's.

Right:
Molded tobacco storage jar, yellow earthenware with Rockingham glaze, unmarked, c. 1850-1880's.

Both tobacco jars or humidors originally had lids that have been lost over the century since they were molded.

Right:
Molded yellow earthenware pitcher with Rockingham glaze, unmarked, c. mid-19th century.

Left:
Molded pitcher, yellow earthenware with Rockingham glaze, unmarked, c. second half of the 19th century.

Right:
Molded yellow earthenware jar with Rockingham glaze. second half of the 19th century.

Below:
Molded yellow earthenware sugar bowls with Rockingham glaze, c. second half of the 19th century.

Left:
Oversized molded yellow earthenware pitcher with Rockingham glaze, bulbous bottom, c. second half of the 19th century.

Right:
Molded yellow earthenware pitcher with Rockingham glaze, c. second half of the 19th century.

Left:
Rockingham molded pitcher, c. 1870's.

Right:
Rockingham molded pitcher, c. 1870's.

Yellowware

The yellowware pictures and information in this section were provided by Barry and Lisa McAllister of 14521 National Pike, Clear Spring, Maryland 21722. The McAllisters are nationally known dealers who specialize in yellowware and other ceramics.

Dinner Plates, 1840-1920

These are quite rare. Apparently they were not too popular when first produced and therefore not many were made. Condition would not be a major factor when buying due to their degree of scarcity.

Above:
Thick, crude plate with the name "Erna" in black slip under the glaze. Probably made for a wife or sweetheart.

Above:
Reticulated-edge plate impressed "Leeds Pottery" on the back. A rare mark for yellowware.

Coffee Pot or "Biggin," 1925-1950

This coffee pot comes with four pieces. The top (with attached filter), the bottom, the lid, and a cover for the filter. These are not too popular yet, due to their late form. They are not common but can be found.

Left:
Coffee Pot or "Biggin."

Mugs, 1840-1930

Mugs are found in a variety of forms and with many different types of decorations. They are very popular with collectors and prices on them are rising steadily. They are not commonly found and minor damage is acceptable on the ones with more unusual decoration.

Above:
Unusual slip and mocha combination.

Below:
Mocha-decorated mugs.

Above:
Slip-decorated mugs.

Storage Crocks, 1840-1920

These are generically called butter crocks but were actually used to store a number of things like sugar, flour, and tobacco. The later banded crocks are fairly easy to find. Some of them will have lost their lids. The mocha or fancy slip decorated pieces are quite rare and should not be passed up if found without lids or with minor damage.

Left:
Cookie jar.

Below:
Rare earthworm deco-rated crock with lid.

Unusual slip-decorated crock with domed lid.

Rare slip-decorated crock with lid.

Above:
Banded crocks with lids.

Above:

Rare slip-decorated crock without lid.

Unusual slip-decorated crock without lid.

Rare earthworm decorated crock without lid.

Above:
Banded crocks with lids.

Above:
Sugar bowls (on each end) with blue seaweed mocha.

Blue seaweed-covered tub for butter or tobacco.

Rolling Pin, 1870-1900

Rolling pins are very popular and never seem to last long before they disappear into someone's collection. They are not common, but wait for a perfect one unless price is the primary factor. Missing wooden handles affect the price only minimally since they can be replaced.

Below:
Yellowware rolling pin.

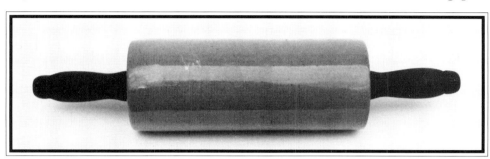

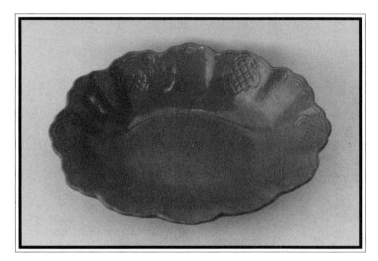

Baking or Serving Dishes, 1840-1900

These very plain pieces of yellowware are very practical. They were the predecessor of today's modern oven-to-table dinnerware. Wear on the bottom (from the oven) and on the inside (from being scraped with spoons) is common. They can still be found with some effort. Baking dishes are very popular, and prices have risen.

Left:
Rare scalloped and embossed server.

Right:
Oval baker impressed "T.G. Green" (England).

Below:
Rare shallow server impressed "American Pottery Co., N.Y."

Below, Right:
Nest of three oval baking dishes.

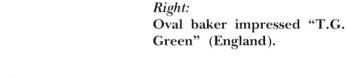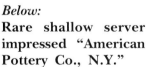

Washboard, 1870-1880

This is an extremely rare item because few were made. They were easily damaged and not practical for household use. Condition is not of paramount importance. It is important that the washboard is yelloware and not stoneware or redware with a yellow overglaze.

Left:
Yellowware washboard.

Keelers, 1870-1920

These were used for storing milk and are rarely found with a lid.

Right:
Plain Keeler.

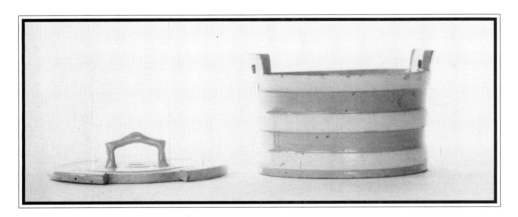

Left:
White banded keeler with a matching lid.

Right:
Flared keeler with brown slip bands.

Custard Cups, 1850-1930

These little cups are popular with collectors. Some try to get one of each different style they find. Others collect them in sets of four to eight. The plain ones are the earliest. Collectors should try to buy them in as good a condition as possible because they are still available in quantity.

Below:
Plain yellow custard cup.

Slip-decorated custard cup.

Sponge-decorated custard cups.

Pitchers, 1840-1940

Pitchers could also make an entire collection by themselves. Pitchers can be found from about 3" to 14" tall in a variety of forms and with many different types of decoration. When buying the later plain or sparsely banded pitchers, try to get them in as good condition as possible since they can be found fairly easily. They are thick walled and have a generally clunky, primitive appearance. Earlier pieces are more graceful and have generous decoration. Damage is more acceptable on examples with rare decoration.

Left:
Rare plain yellowware pitcher with peacocks.

Above:
Graduated set of three blue-banded pitchers.

Above:
Banded and plain pitchers.

Right:
Early banded classic form pitcher.

Very unusual "corn" pitcher.

Weller (Ohio) banded pitcher.

Above:
Rare miniature banded pitchers only 3" tall. The one on the right would have been part of a set with a miniature wash bowl.

Below:
Very large pitcher with blue floral seaweed decoration.

Above:
Rare green and brown bi-colored mocha pitcher.

Unusual pitcher with black seaweed on a creamy yellow slip band.

Below:
Rare mocha thistle pitcher.

Rare blue and black mocha pitcher.

Novelties & Miniatures, 1850-1940

These pieces are representative of the imagination that went into producing pottery. The best thing about collecting yellowware is that it was made in more forms than any other pottery. None of these pieces are commonly found. Some damage would be acceptable considering their degree of rarity.

Left:
Cradle and Iron.

Below:
Mini-jugs from Ohio.

Above:
Swan Toothpick Holder, Tiny Crock, Small Basket and Bank.

Above:
Syllabub or tea cup.

Above:
**Rundlet, Miniature Covered
Casserole, Reamer and Shoe.**

Below:
Large Basket.

Right:
Possibly a snuff jar decorated
with a blue seaweed mocha.
Rare form.

Left:
Small tub with lid and heart-
shaped cutouts in handles.

91

Above:
Doll size, three-piece tea set.

Above:
Possibly a measure or scoop.
The exact purpose of this
English piece is still unknown.
The bar across the center
would seem to be a handle
and the extended rim would
serve as a pouring spout.
Deep brown slip bands add
to the value of the piece.

Right:
Dog doorstop with blue overglaze.

Lion doorstop.

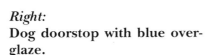

Ladle, 1860-1880

Ladles are extremely
rare and almost impossible
to find. Should you have a
chance to purchase one, do
not let condition be a factor.
They were probably experi-
mental and copies from iron-
stone ladles of the same period.

Left:
Yellowware Ladle.

Teapots, 1830-1930

These are a real favorite with yellowware collectors. In plain yellow and with slip or mocha decoration, they are not easy to find. The latter two are quite rare. You will find many more Rockingham decorated teapots than any other kind. Expect damage on the spout and lid area of a teapot. Should you be lucky enough to be offered a mocha decorated teapot, do not let condition be a major factor in your decision to purchase.

Below:
Rebecca at the Well teapot.

Rare Rebecca teapot with blue oxide overglaze.

Plain yellow teapot with blackberry and basket weave molding.

Above:
Green and brown drip glaze teapot.

Acorns, oak leaves and basket weave molded teapot marked "J.E. Jeffords, Phila."

Plain yellow basket weave teapot.

Left:
Rare floral seaweed teapot.

Extremely rare earthworm decorated miniature teapot.

Pitchers

Above:
Five graduated stoneware pitchers, "Sleepy Eye," Monmouth, Illinois, molded, c. first quarter of the 20th century.

Left:
Blue transfer-decorated pitcher, c. 1850.

Above:
Stoneware milk pitchers, undecorated, c. third quarter of the 19th century.

Left:
Contemporary stoneware pitcher from the Beaumont Pottery, detailed slip-trailed scene of a village, c. 1985.

Right:
Ruckels Pottery pitcher, c. early 20th century.

Above:
Molded stoneware pitchers and mugs, c. early 1900's, White Hall Pottery (Illinois), Bristol interiors, embossed decoration.

Below:
Molded White Hall pitchers, embossed decoration, Bristol interiors, c. first quarter of the 20th century.

Embossing is a process of decoration that was completed as the piece was shaped in the mold. The decoration was not applied later to the piece with slip.

Above:
Pitchers from Ruckels Pottery, White Hall, Illinois, c. first quarter of the 20th century, molded.

Left:
Salt-glazed stoneware pitcher, brushed decoration, thrown on a potter's wheel, unmarked, c. 1860's.

Above:
Spongeware pitcher, molded stoneware, unmarked, midwestern, c. early 1900 s.

Unmarked butter crock, blue transfer-printed decoration, midwestern, c. 1915.

Left:
Rare pancake batter jug, brush dated "1871," replaced bail handle, probably Pennsylvania in origin.

Above:
Batter jug, c. late 19th century, bail handle, Bristol glaze and a molded "platform" jug, c. early 1900's, Bristol glaze.

Molded Pitchers

There are an incredible variety of pitchers that collectors can find. Most of the pitchers are molded and many are unmarked.

Molded pitchers with embossed decorations of flowers, trees, animals, farm scenes, geometric patterns, and people are eagerly sought after by collectors. The pitchers were used on the dinner table for milk, water and cider.

Molded pitchers were made in huge quantities in Ohio, West Virginia, and Illinois potteries from the 1880's through the first quarter of the 20th century.

It is important to note that stoneware pitchers were plentiful, inexpensive, and utilitarian. They were in daily use and few have survived without some blemish.

Above:
Sleepy Eye pitcher, molded with embossed decoration, Monmouth Pottery, Monmouth, Illinois.

Above and Right:
Sleepy Eye pitcher, molded, c. first quarter of the 20th century.

99

Right:
Bristol glaze pitcher with sponge decoration, c. early 1900's.

Below:
Bristol glaze pitcher with sponge decoration, c. 1900.

Below:
Sponge decorated stoneware pitchers, c. 1890-1915.

Above:
"Windmill" embossed decoration, Bristol glaze, molded, unmarked.

Below:
Molded pitcher with embossed flower, sponge decoration, Bristol glaze, c. early 1900's.

Above:
Embossed cow on molded stoneware pitcher, unmarked, c. early 1900's.

Below:
Embossed Dutch boy and girl on molded stoneware pitcher, c. early 1900's.

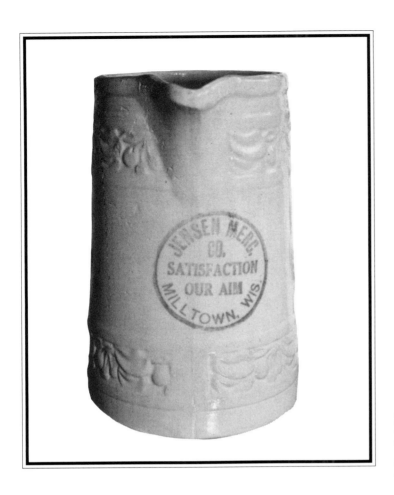

Left and Below:
Molded stoneware pitcher
with embossed decoration
and stenciled vendor's label,
unmarked, c. 1890.

Above:
Bristol glazed pitcher, blue shading, unmarked, c. early 1900's.

Above:
Molded stoneware pitcher, c. early 1900's, unmarked.

Molded Stoneware and Yellowware

Above:
**Yellowware mixing bowl, c.
1900-1940, molded decorated
with slip bands, unmarked.**

Yellowware mixing bowls were made by numerous companies in sizes ranging from 4" to 14".

Below:
**Yellowware mixing bowl, c.
1900-1940, unmarked.**

Right:
Collection of utilitarian yellowware and stoneware from the late 19th/early 20th centuries.

Left:
Molded stoneware bean pot, White Hall Pottery, White Hall, Illinois, c. first quarter of the 20th century.

Above:
Stoneware bowls from the Ruckels Pottery, c. first quarter of the 20th century.

Below:
Stoneware advertising or premium bowls, White Hall Pottery, c. 1900.

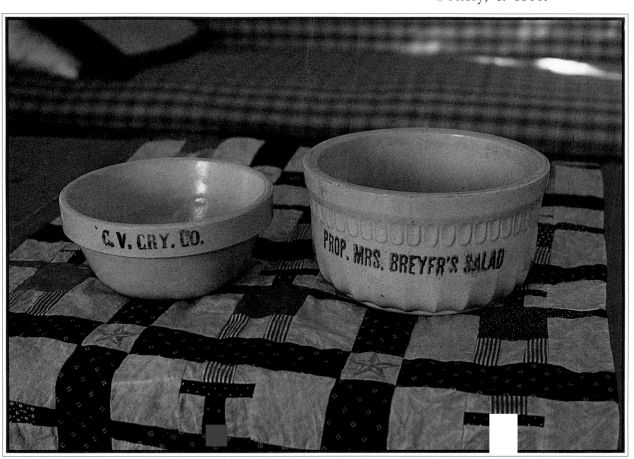

Left:
Stoneware Spaniel, Ebey Pottery, c. 1890.

Many companies made stoneware spaniels to be used as doorstops or decorative pieces for the mantel. Rarely is an example marked.

Next Page:
Rare molded stoneware birdhouse, White Hall Pottery, c. first quarter of the 20th century.

Sewer-tile pottery was made in the late 19th century in Ohio, New York and Pennsylvania.

Right:
Stoneware sewer-tile planter, unmarked possibly from New York state, c. 1890-1915.

Above:
Stoneware butter crocks, c. early 1900's-1920.

Embossed crock with bail handle and maple grip.

"Butter" crock with wire handle.

Right:
Bristol glaze butter crock, bail handle, embossed decoration, c. first quarter of the 20th century.

Left:
Slop jar, bail handle, Bristol glaze, c. first quarter of the 20th century.

Below:
Spongeware covered storage jar, unmarked, c. first quarter of the 20th century.

Above:
Stoneware flag holder, embossed, used in a school or lodge hall, White Hall Pottery, c. early 1900's.

112

Left and Below:
Stoneware storage piece, embossed decoration, "Bread," White Hall Pottery, c. early 1900's, Bristol glaze.

Above:
Stoneware foot warmers, New York state, c. 1880-1910.

Bottles, Flasks and Mugs

Above:
Salt-glazed stoneware ginger beer or sarsaparilla bottles, wheel-thrown, c. 1860-1880.

Left:
Stoneware flask, c. 1830-1860, unmarked and decorated, wheel-thrown.

Below:
Molded "Sleepy Eye" mugs, Monmouth Pottery, Monmouth, Ill., c. first quarter of the 20th century.

115

Glossary

The following terms are basic to any pottery collector's vocabulary.

Albany slip – Brown clay from the Hudson River mixed with water to glaze the interior of stoneware crocks, jugs, churns and jars. It was also commonly used on the exteriors of late 19th century/early 20th century stoneware.

Blue-bird potter – A part-time potter who only produced his wares during the warm weather months. There were hundreds of these local potters who made crocks, jugs and churns during the first half of the 19th century.

Capacity mark – A number brushed, impressed, slip-trailed, or stenciled onto a piece of stoneware to indicate its size (usually in gallons).

Craze – A crack in the glaze on a piece of pottery.

Earthenware – Utilitarian pieces of pottery made from surface dug red clays and fired at about 1700 degrees F. The earthenware products were not water tight and broke easily.

Greenware – Formed and dried pots ready to be put into the kiln for firing.

Incised – A mark or decoration scratched into the surface of a piece of pottery with a sharp tool or piece of wire.

Impressed – A decorative technique used by potters to put simple designs and capacity or maker's marks into the stoneware much like footprints are left on a beach.

Marked – A term that generally refers to the pottery name and location impressed into the piece of stoneware. A piece that is unmarked does not carry the maker's name.

Molded – Not thrown on a potter's wheel. Clay poured into a mold with each piece exactly like every other, not handcrafted.

Ovoid – Term used to describe crocks, churns, and jugs with broad shoulders tapering to a smaller base. A typical ovoid piece was made prior to 1850. After that date, pieces tended to have a gradually more cylindrical form. Could also be described as "pear-shaped."

Peeling or flaking – A process of gradual deterioration usually caused by poor bonding in the kiln with the glaze "flaking" away over time.

Rockinghamware – Yellowware that has been covered with a manganese based, mottled brown glaze.

Salt glaze – A glaze made from table salt. After being thrown into the heated kiln, the salt vaporizes and covers the exposed pieces that are being fired. The process leaves an "orange peel" surface on the stoneware.

Sgraffito – "scratched-ware" – A decorative technique that involved incising designs into the surface of red ware.

Slip – A mixture of clay and water used to decorate pottery.

Slip-trailed – A decorating technique used with a slip-cup and slip much like a cake decorating tool. A piece that is slip-trailed has a raised surface decoration.

Sprigging – Adding molded decorative pieces of clay to the body of a piece of pottery for an ornamental purpose.

Stoneware – Utilitarian pieces of pottery made from clays fired at approximately 2100-2300 degrees F. Stoneware is durable and holds water without a glaze. It was in common use throughout the entire 19th century and well into the first quarter of the 20th century.

Wheel thrown – Made individually on a potter's wheel rather than machine produced or molded.

Bibliography

A multitude of books have been written about American pottery. We would recommend the books below as essential to a basic library of Americana.

Barret, Richard, *Bennington Pottery and Porcelain*, New York, Bonanza Books, 1958.

Guilland, Harold, *Early American Folk Pottery*, Philadelphia, Chilton Book Co., 1971.

Osgood, Cornelius, *The Jug and Related Stoneware of Bennington*, Rutland, Vermont, Charles E. Tuttle and Co., 1971.

Ramsay, John, *American Potters and Pottery*, Boston, Massachusetts, Cushmand and Flint, 1939.

Raycraft, Carol & Don, *Collector's Guide to Country Stoneware and Pottery*, Paducah, Kentucky, Collector Books, 1985.

Webster, Donald, *Decorated Stoneware of North America*, Rutland, Vermont, Charles E. Tuttle and Co., 1971.

Price Guide

Schroeder's Antiques Price Guide

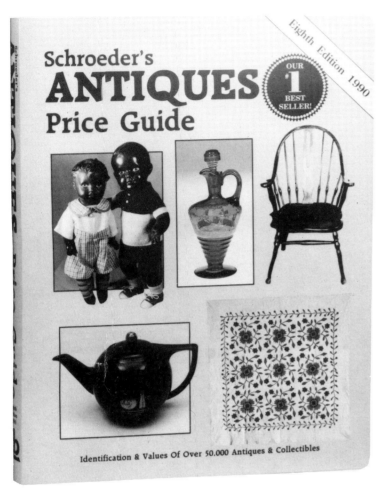

Schroeder's Antiques Price Guide has climbed its way to the top in a field already supplied with several well-established publications! The word is out, *Schroeder's Price Guide* is the best buy at any price. Over 500 categories are covered, with more than 50,000 listings. But it's not volume alone that makes Schroeder's the unique guide it is recognized to be. From ABC Plates to Zsolnay, if it merits the interest of today's collector, you'll find it in Schroeder's. Each subject is represented with histories and background information. In addition, hundreds of sharp original photos are used each year to illustrate not only the rare and the unusual, but the everyday "fun-type" collectibles as well -- not postage stamp pictures, but large close-up shots that show important details clearly.

Each edition is completely re-typeset from all new sources. We have not and will not simply change prices in each new edition. All new copy and all new illustrations make Schroeder's THE price guide on antiques and collectibles.

The writing and researching team behind this giant is proportionately large. It is backed by a staff of more than seventy of Collector Books' finest authors, as well as a board of advisors made up of well-known antique authorities and the country's top dealers, all specialists in their fields. Accuracy is their primary aim. Prices are gathered over the entire year previous to publication, from ads and personal contacts. Then each category is thoroughly checked to spot inconsistencies, listings that may not be entirely reflective of actual market dealings, and lines too vague to be of merit.

Only the best of the lot remains for publication. You'll find *Schroeder's Antiques Price Guide* the one to buy for factual information and quality.

No dealer, collector or investor can afford not to own this book. It is available from your favorite bookseller or antiques dealer at the low price of $12.95. If you are unable to find this price guide in your area, it's available from Collector Books, P. O. Box 3009, Paducah, KY 42001 at $12.95 plus $2.00 for postage and handling.

8½ x 11, 608 Pages $12.95

COLLECTOR BOOKS
A Division of Schroeder Publishing Co., Inc.